Real Hymns,
Real Hymn Books

A Celebration and Invitation

Christopher Idle

Freelance Author and Tutor in Ministry

GROVE BOOKS LIMITED

RIDLEY HALL RD CAMBRIDGE CB3 9HU

Contents

The Author

After thirty years in parish ministry, urban and rural, Christopher Idle works from home in south-east London, involved with local schools and churches, writing and tutoring. His publications include *What Shall We Sing?* (Buxton: Fellowship of Word and Spirit, 1996), *The Word We Preach, The Words We Sing* (Sheffield: Reform, 1998), and *Hymns in Today's Language?* (Grove, 1982—see Introduction). He has contributed to other books and helped to edit five hymnals as well as anthologies and reference works. He is a committee member of the Hymn Society of Great Britain and Ireland, and has addressed its annual Conference (most recently on the hymns of Isaac Watts) and that of its North American counterpart. He edits the quarterly *News of Hymnody* (Grove) and writes for the monthly *New Directions* and *Evangelicals Now*. His own hymn texts were published by St Matthias Press in 1998 as *Light Upon The River*.

The Cover Illustration is by Peter Ashton

First Impression January 2000
ISSN 0144-1728
ISBN 1 85174 423 1

1
Introduction: How Did We Get Here?

This is my second contribution to the Grove Worship series. Like the first, it began with an approach by me, takes hymns for its theme, and almost coincides with the birth of a new hymnal. There the resemblance ends.

To refresh the minds of veterans and to encourage the others, let us briefly revisit 1982. The group of writers, composers and editors who had become Jubilate Hymns was about to launch *Hymns for Today's Church*. Rumours of radical modernizing had reached the Christian press, and later (with the calculated leak by John Capon of a single item beginning *God save our gracious queen*) the secular media as well. Because the book broke new ground, it seemed good to have an *apologia* available separately rather than an extensive preface within it—though the main lines were drawn there, initially in both words-only and full-music editions.

My approach to Grove was received cautiously; I had first to sell the idea of putting our case. The Grove management has positively gloried in the ground-breaking quality of much of its work—'Not the last word, but often the first.' But my score of pages is almost unique in being granted its *imprimatur* on condition that Robin Leaver, then deemed a more respectable name, should write a preface making the broad point that what followed was mostly nonsense.

Unhappily for Robin, one crucial word was lost from his page, and rather lessened the force of his criticism, a fact which he lamented in the fledgling quarterly *News of Hymnody* of which he was the first editor. (Ironically, I became the second, and more recently and almost as suddenly, the fifth.) Other pages also had their casualties, not least because the results of my proof-reading, telephoned from a public call box in Fort William, never reached anyone at all. So mistakes are not hard to find; crucial omissions are less obvious.

All this is past history, except that Robin's final sentence was a precursor of the Grove slogan quoted above, and that *Hymns for Today's Church* (London: Hodder and Stoughton) enjoyed both notoriety and moderate, if not modest, success. The story of its first and second editions (1982 and 1987) may one day be told; here I merely note that imitation is the sincerest form of flattery. Many other editors, committees and hymnals have used our work, with or without acknowledgement, while at the same time savaging the book. The 'updating' issue has been widely debated, and the hidden changes made by most hymnals exposed. If recent editors talk about 'modest,' 'sensible' and 'sensitive' modernizing, we all know who they think is promoting the other sort. If Jubilate became the brand leader for removing archaisms, North American editors were more concerned with inclusive (good) or sexist (bad) language. *HTC*'s first edition touched the edges of this issue; its second, driven and piloted by the tireless Michael Perry, took this further. By American standards we remained hopelessly stuck in the mud.

The pages that follow will glance at the next stage. I find myself writing them after again approaching the publishers, aware that very little had appeared on the subject of hymns since that first foray. Informally encouraged by Hymn Society members, I offered to Grove some material they had heard from me, tailored partly to the millennium. No, came the thoughtful answer; we have no room—but could you please write something entirely different?

After initial reluctance I decided that I could after all add to what has already appeared in the FWS and Reform booklets mentioned above. I stand by these controversial squibs; if I did not think them essential reading I would not have written them. As for *Hymns in Today's Language?* (Grove, 1982, now a collector's item) I might put the case differently today. But I would still put it.

We remain indebted to Robin Leaver for, among other things, his invaluable *Hymns with the New Lectionary* (Grove, 1980) which has now been overtaken by similar lists but which is still a useful resource, not least for its Scripture index. He has written with care about twentieth century hymns, mainly for American publications which are not readily available here. Robin's other 1980 Grove product, *A Hymn Book Survey*, stands out from similar work for its fairness, but now needs an equally balanced successor. This present booklet is less detailed, more impressionist than these thorough listings, and has a different aim. But they are all allies in the same cause of encouraging 'real hymns.'

A word about this title. More will emerge in what follows, but in today's climate a rough and ready measure for a real hymn is that we do not need to sing it twice. Nor does it need similar material to support, extend or amplify it when it appears; like a Psalm or a collect, it is a 'stand-alone' item. In itself, that is no criticism of songs, poems or other contributions, some of them hymn-like, which may work in different ways. Nor is it a value judgment to add that the music of hymns, whether composed before or after the words, usually has a different name attached to it.

My own interest must be declared. I remain committed to the basic Jubilate mindset and stay on their network though I am not a member and cannot speak for those who are. I am not a composer. I have toiled on the initial Jubilate words group planning towards *Sing Glory* (Bury St Edmunds: Kevin Mayhew, 1999) and rather more on the hymnal *Praise!* (Darlington: Praise Trust, 2000) from the Grace Baptists and the Fellowship of Independent Evangelical Churches. As I write, both books are delayed (which hymnals are not?) but due soon. For the latter, I was generously received as an Anglican friend and colleague. If I speak warmly of either book, it is not merely through being involved; I got involved through the shared convictions of both groups. For one thing, they believed in real hymns. It is time we started properly.

2
Farewell to a Century

Here is a list of hymns spanning the twentieth century. Because both years and authors are allowed only one entry each, this is not your 'hundred best.' Not all writers can be represented by their best or best known work; some have been squeezed out in the final selection. But the list does show something of the flavour and diversity of recent times.

Year	Hymn	Author
1900	*O Spirit from on high*	J Brownlie
1901	*Where cross the crowded ways of life*	F Mason North
1902	*Judge eternal, throned in splendour*	H Scott Holland
1903	*O God of earth and altar*	G K Chesterton
1904	*Thine be the glory*	R B Hoyle
1905	*Jesus himself drew near*	A R Habershon
1906	*He who would valiant be*	P Dearmer, after J Bunyan
1907	*For the might of thine arm we bless thee*	C Sylvester Horne
1908	*In Christ there is no east or west*	W A Dunkerley (J Oxenham)
1909	*All creatures of our God and King*	W H Draper, after Francis of Assisi
1910	*In the quiet consecration*	C Coote
1911	*O the deep, deep love of Jesus*	S T Francis
1912	*Be thou my vision*	E H Hull, after M E Byrne
1913	*Lord and Master, who hast called us*	F M Smith
1914	*O breath of life, come sweeping through us*	E A P Head
1915	*Give me, O Christ, the strength that is in thee*	H C Carter
1916	*Lift high the cross*	M R Newbolt, after G W Kitchin

1917	*O Father, for this little life*	G White
1918	*O dearest Lord, thy sacred head*	H E Hardy
1919	*Teach me thy way, O Lord*	B M Ramsey
1920	*Speak, Lord, in the stillness*	E M Grimes
1921	*Father eternal, Ruler of creation*	L Housman
1922	*God is love; let heaven adore him*	T Rees
1923	*Great is thy faithfulness*	T O Chisholm
1924	*Fairest Lord Jesus*	L S Stevenson (from the German)
1925	*Morning has broken*	E Farjeon
1926	*A man there lived in Galilee*	S T C Lowry
1927	*All poor men and humble*	K E Roberts
1928	*Now the green blade riseth*	J M C Crum
1929	*I cannot tell why he whom angels worship*	W Y Fullerton
1930	*Christ is the king! O friends, rejoice*	G K A Bell
1931	*Lord of all hopefulness*	J Struther (J Placzek)
1932	*Let hearts awaken, now the night is ended*	C S Phillips, after Gregory or Alcuin
1933	*Lord of good life, the hosts of the undying*	G Hoyland
1934	*Thou who wast rich beyond all splendour*	F Houghton
1935	*Here, Lord, we take the broken bread*	C V Pilcher
1936	*When Easter to the dark world came*	W H Hamilton
1937	*O day of God, draw nigh*	R B Y Scott
1938	*All praise to thee, for thou, O King divine*	F Bland Tucker
1939	*Sunset to sunrise changes now*	H C Robbins, after Clement of Alexandria
1940	*We would extol thee, ever-blessed Lord*	J N Grieve
1941	*Jesus the Lord said, I am the bread*	C D Monahan (trad)
1942	*Thee we praise, High Priest and Victim*	W Robinson
1943	*Father, although I cannot see*	J Eddison
1944	*Lord of creation, to thee be all praise*	J C Winslow
1945	*Not far beyond the sea*	G B Caird
1946	*We come, O Christ, to thee*	E M Clarkson
1947	*Lord, save thy world: in bitter need*	A F Bayly
1948	*God of the pastures, hear our prayer*	T C Hunter Clare
1949	*O Lord my God, when I in awesome wonder*	S K Hine, after C Boberg
1950	*Ye that know the Lord is gracious*	C A Alington
1951	*Lord, you have searched and known my ways*	P G Jarvis
1952	*God has spoken by his prophets*	G W Briggs
1953	*Where restless crowds are thronging*	T C Clark
1954	*Thanks to God whose word was spoken*	R T Brooks

1955	*God of the fertile fields*	G Harkness
1956	*Worship, glory, praise and honour*	M A P Wood
1957	*O day of joy and wonder*	V N Buchanan
1958	*Lord Jesus Christ, you have come to us*	P R N Appleford
1959	*Help us, O Lord, to learn*	W W Reid
1960	*A stable lamp is lighted*	R Wilbur
1961	*Tell out, my soul, the greatness of the Lord*	T Dudley-Smith
1962	*The Son of God proclaim*	B E Bridge
1963	*Creator of the earth and skies*	D W Hughes
1964	*Christ triumphant*	M J Saward
1965	*Go forth and tell! O church of God, awake!*	J E Seddon
1966	*All who love and serve your city*	E R Routley
1967	*Forgive our sins as we forgive*	R E Herklots
1968	*I come with joy to meet my Lord*	B A Wren
1969	*We have a gospel to proclaim*	E J Burns
1970	*Reap me the earth as a harvest to God*	L Connaughton
1971	*Lord, as I wake I turn to you*	W B Foley
1972	*When in our music God is glorified*	F Pratt Green
1973	*The kingdom of God is justice and joy*	B A Rees
1974	*Father eternal, Lord of the ages*	G B Timms
1975	*Nothing in all creation*	T C Micklem
1976	*Morning glory, starlit sky*	W H Vanstone
1977	*You satisfy the hungry heart*	O Westendorf
1978	*Can man by searching find out God*	E Cosnett
1979	*Born in song*	B Hoare
1980	*He gave his life in selfless love*	C Porteous
1981	*O God beyond all praising*	M A Perry
1982	*Like the murmur of the dove's song*	C P Daw
1983	*You, O Lord, have searched and known me*	D G Preston
1984	*We are marching in the light of God*	A Nyberg (trad)
1985	*The hands that first held Mary's child*	T H Troeger
1986	*Where shepherds lately knelt*	J J Vadja
1987	*Before the world began*	J L Bell and G Maule
1988	*Put peace into each other's hands*	F H Kaan
1989	*How long, O Lord, how long*	A H F Luff
1990	*Come, you people of the promise*	J F Patterson
1991	*May heaven's Guardian be praised*	S Horsfall, after Caedmon
1992	*Dark the night, but joy comes in the morning*	P Wigmore
1993	*Beauty for brokenness*	G Kendrick
1994	*Forgive, forgive us, holy God*	S E Murray
1995	*Born of Adam, torn from Eden*	H Jolly

1996	*Christ, when we cling to false security*	A Gaunt
1997	*Teach me, dear Lord, to savour every moment*	M E Leckebusch
1998	*Light a candle for thanksgiving*	D Mowbray
1999	*O God, enthroned in majesty*	M Forster
2000	*See, a New Year lies ahead*	A R Ingleby
	(see *News of Hymnody* 73, January 2000)	

There at a glance is the century of our birth. Which enterprising publisher will issue these hundred (and one) as a souvenir of times past? The list needs some warning labels. The dates are not infallible. Some are well-authenticated years of writing, others, of first known appearance. Some are disputed, others estimated. Some first lines have changed, not to mention second or subsequent ones.

If your favourite author is missing, so are some of mine—Tom Colvin, Ian Fraser and Colin Gibson among them. Some are vague or reticent about the date of writing, or their work may have taken shape in a busy year. Translations and adaptations are included; the list takes account of writers outside Britain, but I have tried not to make it eccentric. Some items are on the edges of 'real' hymnody, and their appearance here is not an accolade for quality. But the fact that some first lines (and authors) remain almost unknown does not indicate inferiority; some classics have taken a century or two to become established. An overlapping musical exercise would be revealing.

One reaction may be that the century has not done too badly, even before the song-writing explosion of the 1960s. What is wrong with some of these lasting treasures from the 1950s and before? Many of my hundred look at least as healthy as the Victorian list provided in Ian Bradley's book *Abide With Me* (London: SCM, 1997)—which was not restricted to one per year or per author. All such lists have obvious limits.

But they hint at the wealth of human resources, theological exploration, committed devotion, doctrinal fashion, church dynamics, publishing trends—the social, national and world events which have shaped them. Without claiming to provide a definitive summary of a hundred years of hymns, let us take some soundings here and there, in the form of just seven of the texts.

These are in no way my 'top seven,' but (to change the metaphor) they may well be windows opening out on wider horizons—like the other 93. Most are readily accessible, but even without the text in front of you, the reader, I hope that my comments will make sense. If you will excuse the 17th century language, 'A man who looks on glass, on it may stay his eye; or, if he pleaseth, through it pass, and then the heaven espy.'

3
Stories and Snapshots

1. Starting At The End: On The Throne, Or In The Gutter?
O God, enthroned in majesty: Michael Forster 1999

It may be ironic to close our muddled, tortured century with a first line which seems to take sides on one of the great divides of its worship. Put simply: Is God, or Christ, 'still on the throne'—as many older Christians can remember singing from *CSSM/SU Choruses*? Or has this ancient linguistic currency lost all its value?

It was in 1971 that Britain scrapped its shillings and half crowns in favour of the 'new money.' Around that time, too, the waves of 'renewal' songs began washing over the church; for them, sovereigns and crowns were the very things to sing about. But the lyrics rarely gave kingship much content, let alone facing any of the questions it raises. Most of them were put together (and still are) by those who also wrote the tune. Recent publicity for one such collection advertises it as 'experience-driven'; it might be truer to say that they are music-driven or even rhythm-driven. This genre hardly surfaces in my list, not simply because most of it fails to meet the criteria for 'real hymns,' but because its own exponents would resist any such categorization. But one of its most obvious features is the triumphalism of such repeated themes as majesty, victory, winning battles and defeating enemies, claiming territory, raising banners, asserting power, and so on. Repetition often aids the victory mood; it is more enjoyable to rerun our triumphs than our laments.

At the other end of the scale is the volume of texts which specifically avoid and even deny any such desire to dominate and 'win.' A near-perfect example is my 1976 choice, W Hubert Vanstone's *Morning glory, starlit sky*— in its revised form which while available in many books may now be illegal to reprint. At first sight, Vanstone and Forster represent two irreconcilable opposites. I think, and regret, that Vanstone's masterpiece emphasizes his point so far as to cause many editors to take fright, and play safe. Not many books include it. Others might respond that to qualify or try to balance his striking paradoxes would destroy not just the poetry but the hymn itself. It would be like asking Amos to be slightly more tactful in his attack on the Jewish sacrificial system to avoid any possible misunderstandings by literal-minded priests.

But Vanstone is simply the finest of a swarm of writers who are all keen to steer us away from thrones, monarchs, majesty and perhaps heaven itself. It is bad enough to have to spend so long in 'worship' of this sort; an even greater problem is the unrealistic nature of the claims made by so many of the words. To assert that everything is wonderful when jobs are lost, children die, fear rules the streets or the church is split, is a form of denial close to saying 'I am healed' when plainly I am not. It has nothing in common with the biblical realism and genuine victories of Romans 8, 2 Corinthians 6, Hebrews 11, or those parts of Revelation which many lyrics superficially echo.

Some will reply along these lines: in the world, from Monday to Saturday, everything is against us—notably if we live in certain areas, work in certain jobs (or none) or have skin of a certain colour. Come Sunday, we can at last dress in our finery (unlike those rich young Christians who ostentatiously 'dress down' for church), join with our true brothers and sisters, and shout the praises of God who really is in control in spite of appearances to the contrary.

I hope we can all see both sides of this tension, and maybe experience them. It is not usually those who live among concrete who want to sing about it on Sunday. Many urban-reality hymns from the sixties onwards were written from paternalistic professional heights rather than street-level anxieties.

So I come back to Michael Forster—not to a classic hymn in the Vanstone class but to a recent one which just gets it right. 'Enthroned in majesty'—that still needs to be said. It is part of our faith. But see how it continues: 'crowned with mortal pain...no cheap and easy formula...none stands blameless...the crosses of the world.' In a note to another text, this author has written 'the "triumph" here is over triumphalism itself...Far from exceeding the kind of majesty the world recognized, Jesus simply, humbly, painfully puts it to shame for the sham it is' (*The Hymns of Michael Forster*, Bury St Edmunds: Kevin Mayhew 1998, p 32). In terms of yet another, we need not be ashamed of proclaiming 'Christ triumphant' provided we also include its third stanza: 'Suffering servant, scorned, ill-treated...' Triumph is usually more popular than servanthood.

2. Moving to the Centre: Birth of a Classic, Death of a Culture?
Tell out, my soul, the greatness of the Lord: **Timothy Dudley-Smith 1961**

It should be clear from a glance through my chosen hundred that we cannot precisely date the start of the 'hymn explosion.' Like others, I prefer different metaphors; our new century may provide some. But explosions, like concrete, have marked recent decades, and this word is widely applied to hymns in English from—well, when? Patrick Appleford could justly claim to be a pioneer. But Albert Bayly, George Bell, George Caird and 'Jan Struther' were writing fresh-sounding texts long before 1950. Much is rightly claimed for the *Dunblane Praises* which advanced from 1962 in strikingly creative directions, and some have even announced themselves as hymnic Luthers of the 1960s. Much was happening, and changing, at about the same time. What can hardly be doubted is that one of the century's finest books about hymns is *The English Hymn* (Oxford: Clarendon Press, 1997), where Prof J R Watson cites *Tell out, my soul* as the 'detonator' for the explosion, which 'helped to create a micro-climate for modern hymn-writing' (pp 28 and 345).

If I may comment on the work of Bishop Timothy, to whom personally I owe so much, I feel that this exhilarating text is not his best. Nor has it yet found its ideal tune (WOODLANDS is also exhilarating, but not when it puts 'my soul' on its top note!). It is no great compliment to rate a writer's first hymn his finest—is it downhill all the way thereafter? Three recent polls, admittedly small scale, put *Lord, for the years* level, or ahead; other candidates from this source make the field extremely crowded.

But another aspect of the story is less noticed. *Tell out, my soul* appeared first in the *Anglican Hymn Book* (London: Church Book Room Press, 1965) from the publishing arm of Church Society. This was the flagship, all too briefly, for evangelical Anglicans—almost a party badge, and a reassuringly bright feature of their flagship churches. It often replaced ageing copies of *The Church Hymnal for the Christian Year* (London: Novello/Marshall Brothers, 1917) which was still in use in my curacy days.

The editors did not get the tune right, but that could be said of much of their music. Thirty-five years on it is remarkable how much dead wood the book contains (almost as much as the latest *Mission Praise*); at the time, it seemed to be the natural successor both to *CHCY* and to the *Hymnal Companion* to the *Book of Common Prayer* (London: Longmans, Green; 1870–1890, still reprinting in 1954). These were seen as evangelical 'party' books only because so much Anglicanism had departed from its roots. The all-but-all-conquering *Hymns Ancient and Modern* (in its 1922 or 1950 editions) now occupied the centre ground in spite of so much which was extra-biblical and non-Prayer Book.

What *AHB*'s editors could not know was that while they gathered up George Briggs, George Caird, Margaret Clarkson, Frank Houghton, Bryn Rees, and Timothy Dudley-Smith, they were just too early, too highbrow, or both, to catch the wind blowing through *Youth Praise* (London: Falcon, 1966 and 1969), plus Dunblane, Appleford, Beaumont and all. In 1978 some 'additional hymns' of mixed quality were oddly tacked on at the front, but soon after Oxford University Press took over publication in the 1980s, it dropped from their lists. But this was not before a small group which I chaired had produced *Anglican Praise* (Oxford: OUP, 1987), a 100-hymn supplement commissioned by Church Society who after it appeared promptly lost interest. Other battles seemed more urgent; who can say they were wrong?

Let us backtrack a bit. With *AHB* still less than ten years old, the group which became Jubilate Hymns, and which itself emerged from *Psalm Praise* (London: Falcon, 1973), began planning a more radical hymn book. Some of us had no desire to rival, let alone sink, the *AHB*; the 'we' passages continue here, as I laboured from the Jubilate side to bring together the continuing *AHB* editors and those working towards *Hymns for Today's Church*. We had clear differences, mainly over how far to take the process of modernizing older texts. One committee feared dumbing-down; the other, exclusive addiction to Radio 4 words and Radio 3 music. But we did not divide neatly; some in either group would have been as happy in the other. The tragedy of these years was a clash of personalities, despite efforts of senior evangelical statesmen to help us produce one book instead of two.

One book did finally emerge—but it was 'ours,' in 1982—a flawed product in terms of balance of authors, hurried indexing, and a last-minute 'song section' making little long-term sense (perhaps the one point I share with John Leach's booklet W 132 *Hymns and Spiritual Songs*). But it did concentrate the minds of many beyond our own constituency, and beyond Britain, on the question of updating. For some it was a signpost; to others, a boundary-fence; to others, a danger signal. For most, at least it made an impact.

What of the *AHB* successors? In time they severed their links with Church Society, as our group did with the Church Pastoral Aid Society; from the hymnbook side (both of them) it felt like a push rather than a jump. With Canon Herbert Taylor at the helm, succeeded by Geoffrey Whitehead, they had originally planned a major revision of *AHB*, but came to see that a new book was the only way to recognize the best of the 'explosion.' They actually produced a book—words and music complete, in ring binders. In the 1980s climate, no-one would publish. By an extraordinary twist of events, the main files came to me, on the untimely death of the now disillusioned chairman, Geoffrey Whitehead. I worked through box after box of text, correspondence, minutes, music, and, yes, revisions. I had no claim to any of this, but only my intervention saved it from the dustcart.

To conclude this tragi-comedy, when *Sing Glory* was in preparation, I hoped that some of our team would share the task of preserving the best work of Geoffrey and his committee. Alas, no. A tiny group of their hymns survived our own sifting, and a higher editorial tier pruned this selection yet further. When Church Society invited me to its 1998 Conference, I concluded my address by presenting its then director with one heavy box, the hard-copy heart of the Taylor-Whitehead legacy. With one exception; I trusted only myself, for now, to retain Geoffrey's meticulous notes on every hymn in *AHB*. He was a painstakingly accurate researcher; eventually his three handwritten books must find a permanent home. With sadly accidental irony, I find myself preparing this booklet on paper salvaged from the ruins of what would have been *Hymns for Worship*.

We have travelled a long way from *Tell out, my soul*. In changing times, Jubilate lives on, no longer so keen as it once was to disown its *Youth Praise* roots. But *Sing Glory* is a new direction altogether. The tradition of Edward Bickersteth, Victoria Carbery, Herbert Taylor and Geoffrey Whitehead, wedded to reverent evangelical liturgy, the Bible, the Lord's Supper, and the *Book of Common Prayer*, has gone out with the twentieth century. It made a good and godly contribution. Occasionally a tremor of its death-throes is heard, as in the *Companion to Hymns and Psalms* (Peterborough: Methodist Publishing House, 1988). Fred Pratt Green's *Pray for the church, afflicted and oppressed*, we read on p 327, 'was written in response to an appeal by the editor of a projected Anglican book, not in fact published.' Happily, the hymns of Timothy Dudley-Smith and Fred Pratt Green live on.

3. Further Back: Focus for Unity?
Christ is the king! O friends, rejoice: **George K A Bell 1930**

Many ways of defining hymns have been tried. Rather than add to the many boundary lines already marked out, let us put our hymns to work. What can they do?

It is easy to point to hymns and hymnbooks which by accident or design are divisive. In addition to their devotional and teaching value (or sometimes detracting from it) they act as a flag-waving ritual, a team-building, morale-boosting song closer to football chanting than their supporters would admit. The Wesley brothers with their militant Arminianism must take some responsibility here; not the first, but some of the most famous.

The inspiring title of John Wesley's 1741 *Hymns on God's Everlasting Love* (long before the definitive 1780 book) disguises for modern readers the fact that its aim was largely polemical—not to counter the devil and all his works, but George Whitefield and many of his. To support his published sermons and tracts against Calvinism, John issued hymns by brother Charles which spelled out with eloquence and wit the case against the doctrines of election and predestination. No writer can have used the word 'all,' pressed to its extreme limits, to better effect. Later he did a similar job for 'plead,' 'sacrifice' and 'perfect.'

Such hymns as these do nothing to heal; ironically, the more we know of their background, the less use they are today. When Reformed churches revise them, as for instance in *Christian Hymns* (Bridgend: Evangelical Movement of Wales, 1977), they prolong their lives but attract the wrath of the hymn-antiquarians whose chief interest lies in the original text.

A recent Roman Catholic writer cannot expect everyone to join in his rousing (and closing) couplet: 'Be with our world, its only hope; be with your church, be with our Pope.' Yes, we all find 'hope' a problematic rhyme in English; archbishops, moderators and conference presidents do not fit hymnody so neatly. Songs about the 'queen of heaven' and 'sinless Eve' may help to rally the massed ranks of Rome, but have an equally limited usefulness.

We encounter songs from the edge of the Spring Harvest scene whose author-composers are in no doubt what we should be doing, and expecting God to do. The demand for signs is not new, but the emphasis in the lyrics is clearly meant to divide the renewed from the stale, the filled from the feeble. Some hymns designedly exclude infants from the ordinance of baptism; or spin out ideas of eucharistic sacrifice or real presence in terms hardly suited to inter-church worship. Others require adherence to particular policies and fashions, or even rehearse the arguments for women vicars.

It is not a case of not noticing one's own accent or turn of phrase, like some hopeful sixties' songs about racial harmony which could be sung only by whites, or recent ones about poverty which are usable only if you are rich. It is a matter of deliberate definition and rallying round the tribal flag.

By way of contrast, consider Isaac Watts. Among all his extraordinary achievements, one of the less noticed is this: his hymns are truly, properly, catholic. They are not denominational, still less sectarian or belligerently partisan for his own followers, for he had none. James Montgomery's 19th century tribute bears repeating: 'As the poet of Methodism, Charles Wesley has sung the doctrines of the gospel as they are expounded *among that people* [my italics]…Dr Watts, on the contrary, though a conscientious Dissenter, is so entirely catholic in his hymns that it cannot be discovered from any of them that he belonged to any particular sect (*The Christian Psalmist*, Glasgow, 1825).

This is very different from those bland hymns which say nothing and can be sung by anyone. Watts has doctrinal meat with his verbal melodies; his hymns unite, but on high ground. So, I suggest, do many of the authors appearing in my list, not least Bishop George Bell.

It is not enough, these days, to say 'brothers' unless you are being literal, as in 'all Joseph's brothers.' It may be counterproductive to say 'sisters and brothers,' since we do not normally reverse a phrase like 'ladies and gentlemen' unless we aim to be awkward. George Bell's text does not sound revolutionary, but he was one of the first to break away from the 'men/brothers/brethren' code of the Victorian hymns. They usually meant to be inclusive and were read and sung as such, but not any more—though today's Americans seem curiously to be getting away with 'you guys.' *Christ is the king* is not now sung exactly as written, in the four 6-line stanzas of *Songs of Praise*, but its heart is unchanged. It was requested, in that extraordinary phrase, 'to carry the tune,' and Percy Dearmer's *Songs of Praise Discussed* (Oxford: OUP, 1933) has no more to say about the text. It is rough justice that the tune has withered while the words flourish.

But even if 'men' survive in two other lines, Bell has 'brothers and sisters' in his opening couplet, and 'O Christian women, Christian men' to begin his original second verse. It is not only in this inclusive language that the hymn passes the Montgomery-Watts test of catholicity; who could guess the source of such a hymn if they did not already know? Some might complain of the final line ('and the whole church at last be one') that the church is *one* already, but those most keen to assert that theological truth have sometimes been responsible for painfully practical splits. More than most, George Bell believed in one holy catholic and apostolic church, and did more than most to reflect his credal position by ground-level action.

That is what hymns at their best can do—even at less than their best. The classics, old or new, have spanned denominational walls as if they did not exist. They also unite at other levels. Some songs, even hymns, cut the writer off from the singing congregation. They preach at those for whom they purport to be written (thank you, Lord, that we are not like those people who ignore the poor), stirring up guilt, self-delusion, or simply resentment. Good hymns express the body's unity, local and universal, and by their 'performative language' do much to enhance, renew, and even create it.

Before coming to other facets of unity, we must see the fences too—or are they warning signs? George Bell famously felt only limited oneness with those who bomb their neighbours. Another Bell, John (born 1949), shares a similar vision of justice and peace—which is another story. The point we must not lose is that while some songs and hymns mouth the slogans and wear the badges of this group or that within Christendom, the greatest hymns may be sung unreservedly by all believers in Christ. The defining boundary, as it is the cutting edge, is the word of the Lord.

4. Not Yet the Future: The International Flavour?
The hands that first held Mary's child: **Thomas H Troeger 1985**

Hymns which can be sung only in their country or culture of origin have a limited value. We curiously welcome some very African or Australian hymns while remaining critical of America-specific or British-oriented texts— or *vice versa*. Recent years have seen a further healthy explosion of Hispanic, Scandinavian and Asian hymnody, recognized for the first time in mainstream North American books but much less so in Britain.

But the most useful hymns, while rich in local flavour, do not offer mementoes or advertise the climate; in circling the globe they transcend barriers of race and place. One author whose recognition 'over here' still lies in the future is Thomas Troeger. The strength of his writing and the force of his language spring directly from the Scriptures which he always unfolds in freshly illuminating ways. His texts hardly surface among the thousands of first lines from British books listed comprehensively in *HymnQuest* (London:

Stainer and Bell, 1997)—which incidentally gives sources for 89 of my 100. (Most of the rest feature on *HymnQuest's* forthcoming CD-ROM; a few remain unpublished). The first-choice tune has not always helped Thomas Troeger, but that does not explain the equal rarity here of Carl Daw, Gracia Grindal, Keith Landis, Jeffrey Rowthorn, Jaroslav Vajda and others.

My 1985 selection arrived in Britain *via New Hymns for the Lectionary* (Oxford: OUP 1986—not to be confused with Robin Leaver's 1980 book; see Introduction). Some of these 52 hymns, while doctrinally straight, may be too linguistically daring, and most have proved too bold for our time. Is it a style whose day will come? I hope so! Compared with the vast amount of 'new' material flooding the churches for thirty years, these probing texts are exquisitely crafted and genuinely fresh pieces of writing, all of them enhancing and illustrating the Scriptures from which they spring.

At first glance this is another 'Mary's child' Christmas lullaby. Far from it! The hands, of course, are masculine: 'The hands that first held Mary's child were hard from working wood.' Here is a superb 'men's hymn' bringing us images not of weapons, battles and brute force, but of tenderness, care, wonder and work. In the Dudley-Smith tradition, it recognizes the mystery of incarnation but does not leave us at Bethlehem. It is poetry which a congregation can sing.

As soon as we use the word 'Bethlehem' or 'Jerusalem' most of us have travelled thousands of miles and encountered a language we cannot read, let alone speak or translate. We are so used to this that we hardly notice. But these 'foreign' particulars bring human beings closer to one another, not further apart. That must be the aim of every hymn which purports to cross other barriers, to celebrate our differences and distances without suggesting superiority or rivalry, let alone hostility. This is a hymn which is not so much American (though it took an American Presbyterian to write it) as human and Christian.

Most congregations, and probably most people who announce hymns, have little idea of the origins of the words they are about to introduce or sing. Some may not even care to know, though in multi-cultural churches this could be culpable ignorance in a minister. Editors have no excuse for such agnosticism, and can enrich those who use their books by brief notes on the hymns. Editors in a new century, please do not miss out on this man!

5. Not Quite the Beginning: The Pilgrims' Way?
He who would valiant be: **Percy Dearmer, after John Bunyan**

This section is not an abridged revamping of my earlier Grove *apologia* (see Introduction). Language, like much else, has moved fast since 1982, but some issues still induce carping among the critics and panic among publishers. In an early product of the 'Dunblane' group, Ian Fraser wrote that 'suggestions for improvements of words should be sent to me.' Isaac Watts and John Ellerton made equally gracious concessions, and Mrs Alexander (what else can we call her?) showed a similar willingness to listen to criticism; Fred Pratt Green likewise.

The octogenarian Fraser, addressing the Hymn Society in 1998, went further. He had no time at all, he said, for people who claimed their words came straight from the Holy Spirit and therefore must not be changed. He might have been talking about some of the current 'renewal' songs; one leading songwriter said he would listen to friendly critics, but if God gave him the words he dared not change them. In fact, in the Scotsman's sights was Hildegard of Bingen, whose medieval feminist star is currently in the ascendant but whose claims to inspiration do not go down well in Dunblane.

How different is the hymn-life of our own dear Mr Wesley! In the oddest part of his 1779 Preface, he says that no-one could possibly change his (and Charles's) words for the better. Even odder, this is still quoted by his admirers as the model attitude! Yet his own Journals and pocket Dictionary show him to be aware of the ebb and flow of language, and the way he messed up other people's verse and prose (notably George Herbert's) was nobody's business—except perhaps the magistrates', since they once fined him for updating hymns without permission.

Today we face other strange phenomena. The writers who seem never content with what they have written, but produce five successive printed versions, each one a response to the latest challenge about race, gender, (dis)ability, and so on. Will animals be next? There can literally be no end to this process. I have felt the pull of it, but there comes a point when most writers say 'There is my text; if it doesn't quite match the mode or fit the current vernacular, then either I must write, or you must find, something different.' I do not apply the phrase 'politically correct' since that is often used pejoratively, to ridicule all change and to defend insensitive or obsolete words which vulnerable people find offensive.

Also strange are the revisers (Jubilate included) who rewrite half of someone else's hymn and then copyright the new version—and say that no-one must revise their revision! The whole principle of updating rests on the premise that no text is sacrosanct; it is the strength of hymns, not their weakness, which enables them to adapt and survive, rather than fossilize and die. Years ago we were advised that copyright was essential to protect our editorial work; whatever the economics of it, such signs deface the text by adding (literally) their own sub-text. This draws attention to all the wrong things and undermines the impact of the hymn.

Which brings us to Bunyan and Dearmer, two men with little in common except one of the best known hymns in the language—largely thanks to MONKS

GATE and Ralph Vaughan Williams. Let us return to *Songs of Praise Discussed*; here (p 271) is Percy Dearmer discussing the original song in John Bunyan's *Pilgrim's Progress*, part 2: 'In 1904, we who were working at the *English Hymnal* felt that some cheerful and manly hymns must be added to the usual repertory [sic]; and this song sprang to mind. It was a daring thing to add [this] song to a hymn book, and it had never been attempted before. To include the hobgoblins would have been to ensure disaster; to ask the congregation of St Ignotus, Erewhon Park, to invite all to come and look at them, if they wished to see true valour, would have been difficult.'

And so on for a further page of Dearmer wit on hobgoblins (he is good on worms, too) bringing in Shakespeare, the Authorized Version, metrical Psalms, and Bunyan himself in defence of his own bold rewriting. Some recent hymnals, notably Baptist ones, have indicated a backlash in favour of hobgoblins (to name the fears and phantoms may help to exorcise them) but Dearmer's radical revision has won its way into countless hymnbooks, churches and school assemblies. Nine out of ten of those able to name any author would mention Bunyan without qualification.

It helped, no doubt, that without Dearmer and Vaughan Williams no-one would be singing Bunyan anyway. Is this a special case? But so, it could be argued, are all the others where changes are necessary for varied reasons—to avoid comedy, unintelligibility or plain inaccuracy. Richard Mant's popular *Bright the vision that delighted* (*Round the Lord in glory seated*) embodies more actual errors of fact in its opening lines than any purportedly Bible-based text I know.

For good measure it stops at the 'alternate hymn' without giving the slightest hint of what 'Judah's seer' was doing listening to it, what happened to him as a result, and why the narrative should be so momentous for his CV, let alone ours. Not even Richard Redhead's glorious tune LAUS DEO can obscure the fact that we truly need an alternate hymn for Isaiah chapter 6. Come back, Percy Dearmer; you pounced on many mistakes, but made no comment on those of Bishop Mant.

The vigour of Bunyan the village tinker has more defenders, and more attraction, than the cultured carelessness of Dr Mant of Winchester, Oxford, and Ireland. I do not arbitrate here between the pilgrim's wind and weather and the editor's defence and disaster. Clearly, however, some changes to original hymns have common sense and public acceptance on their side. Others are long overdue.

6. Behind and Before: Psalms Rediscovered?
You, O Lord, have searched and known me: **David G Preston, 1983**

The latter years of our century have seen many attempts to rediscover the Psalms, or recover them for the churches. This is both good news and bad; it is good news in that somebody cares about their neglect, but bad in highlighting the constant need to remind the church of its foreshortened memory-span.

David Preston, whose friendship and criticism (like that of the late Michael Perry) I have long valued, has given his talents not to work on new texts, but to music, editing and revision, and supremely to Psalm paraphrases which have usually taken years to bring to what he regards as an acceptable form. Even then he will know where there is a weaker line, a phrase he has reluctantly settled on, a word which does not quite carry the required nuance. He is not alone in this; recent Psalm versions include many from Carl Daw, Timothy Dudley-Smith, James Quinn, Jubilate authors in various publications, and several Scots and Canadian authors from the Presbyterian tradition.

But his own work, appearing first in any quantity in *The Book of Praises* (Liverpool: Carey Publications, 1986) should reach a wider public as *Praise!* becomes established, and as the accurate fluency of his versions is appreciated. More important, at least for Free Churches, its resource of a complete metrical Psalter could help to re-establish Psalms not simply as a book for study and preaching, but for singing. This surely is what Paul and Timothy have in mind in those texts from Ephesians (5.19–20) and Colossians (3.16) without which no work on hymns seems complete. And if this book does not prove ideal for Anglicans, they at least have a wealth of other material at their disposal.

As for my particular choice for 1983, Psalm 139 has been claimed (by Kirkpatrick, Kidner, Weiser and others) as one of the most magnificent and penetrating of the 150—though who are we to award prizes to holy Scripture? Unlike many, David Preston's version does not fight shy of the closing verses which confront us with the ugliness of evil and our own reaction to it. Just how far we want to go in *singing* of such things has been widely debated at least since Isaac Watts' famous manifesto on the subject. And if we sing at all as Christians, in what terms shall we sing of judgment and wrath? Many earlier versifiers have been fierce in their zeal to emulate biblical laments and protests; our present tendency would be to resolve such tensions too smoothly. Dancing is in, damnation is out.

I do not claim, any more than he does, that Dr Preston has found the answer denied to his struggling predecessors, but his versions expose the limitations of many 'psalms' which simply evade the difficulty by leaving out the problem verses. I cannot see the original writers accepting that as a legitimate smoothing, or soothing, of their desperate shouts and angry tears. And 'David' is a not unsuitable name for one who wrestles hard to make them both authentic and singable for our own day. If they are not to be identified with real hymns—for they are different—at least they are genuine renderings of the psalms.

There remain many different levels of paraphrase, from the stiffly literal which sacrifice fluency to accuracy and metre, to songs which have only a loose connection with their starting point but which somehow convey the mood of the Psalmist. The 1549 'Old Version' of Sternhold and Hopkins has its jerky inversions excused on the grounds of their faithfulness to the Hebrew; but they were not faithful enough for Ainsworth (1612), nor Ainsworth for the American *Bay Psalm Book* (1640). Some closely literal versions simply do not sound like songs at all; more recent versifications do not always read much like the original David. It is doubtful whether either extreme merits the title 'Psalm.' The best versions remain those in the Bible; failing that, the Prayer Book.

7. Finding the Pattern: Right Person, Right Places?
A Man there lived in Galilee: Somerset T C Lowry 1926

Of my seven 'window' texts, this is the only one to arrive here accidentally. It chose itself simply by starting with 'A,' and would be my number one if the hymns were arranged alphabetically. Why is this worth a comment? Because if choosing hymns is a skilled art, choosing a hymnal can be delightful, draining, or both. One early decision must be whether you want one which is alphabetically arranged. Formerly, the A–Z collections were usually supplements containing anything from twenty to 120. These days, major books of hymns (and songs) are put together in this way. How do we decide between that and other arrangements—credal, liturgical, thematic, the church's year, or Christian experience? In any such list of possible plans, A–Z is the odd one out by a mile.

At first sight, an alphabetical arrangement has much to be said for it. Like other issues it was raised, though not seriously discussed, at early Jubilate meetings. Is it significant if your book starts with *A man there lived in Galilee*? One supplement does just that; another makes it second. It is a useful hymn, and there are many worse ways of opening a collection than this.

'A Man'—in the face of those who by implication deny the humanity or the masculinity of Jesus of Nazareth, that still needs to be said. 'There lived'—these are real historical events. 'In Galilee'—the name is still there, with its lake and river, fields and hills, towns and villages, and places made famous by those who first wrote the story down. His sinlessness is not a prime concern in many modern hymns.

So why not start with whatever hymn begins the alphabet? The texts are easy to trace; it may even save an index. They are no more jumbled up chronologically than by any other method; this is not like a poetry anthology arranged by dates of birth.

If you are ever responsible for choosing hymns, you will know some of the headaches this can cause. Even with a subject index, you have much more rummaging to do. And suppose your subject is not there? To state the obvious but neglected factor: your communion hymns, like your Advent hymns, your evening ones and so on, are scattered randomly through the book. To find them, let alone compare them, takes some doing. In an ideal church, the hymn selection will mean a long search. Because some fall slightly short of perfection, the 'flip through' method is certain to receive a boost from such books. 'We shall sing hymn 106'—because it happened to catch someone's eye on the same page as No 104. There are those who think that does not matter.

If there are drawbacks to the A–Z plan, there are positive gains in other methods. We live in days when some church memories are short; when many (not least those with the alphabetical books or none) reckon that church history began around in 1900, or 1970, or last month. God's people journey through the centuries, not as a train through stations, but as a family growing generations.

It is not just the dates at the foot of the hymn. The whole plan of a book reminds us that where we tread, many others have walked before. Caedmon is on my list. They have taken time to work out their faith, and arrange their singing accordingly. A computer, after all, could do the alphabetical listing, and that is possibly why some have gone for this easier option. They end up not only with inadequate representation of some themes (perhaps the Bible, baptism, the life of Jesus, or world justice) but also *no idea that it is inadequate.* You have to check through every item to find out—if you want to know.

Every 'systematic' arrangement has its drawbacks too; we rarely find a section labelled 'Thanksgiving,' and while some cross-referencing can help, those books which provide seventy pages of indexes tend to daunt rather than help the chooser. But the advantage of seeing our hymns for Easter, or repentance, or heaven, as a group, outweighs most of the snags. We get to find our way round our own books, whereas the A–Z's have no way round to find.

If you have been reading this booklet straight through, you may have been puzzled, even irritated, at the way our seven hymns have dodged around the century and the subjects in no clear order. Exactly. It is good to have a proper arrangement! We can certainly trace some planning in the Book of Psalms—not quite a contents page, but a far more sophisticated system than anyone has yet suggested or researched. The interweaving patterns and clusters of Psalms can be a delight to discover.

If you prefer a simpler rule of thumb in selecting the ideal book for your church, let me offer this. Check through any likely starter and score one mark for every 'yes.'

1   Does it include *The old rugged cross*?
2   Does it have *There is a land of pure delight* and *Give me the wings of faith*?
3   Or *O valiant hearts*?
4   Or *For the fruits of his creation*?
5   Or *When I feel the touch*?
6   Or *Forgive our sins, as we forgive*?
7   Or *City of God, how broad and far*?
8   Or *All glory to God in the sky* and *Glory be to God on high*?
9   Are there plenty of copyright addresses printed under each hymn?
10   Will the music edition stay open, or even stay put, on the piano/organ/keyboard?
11   Does its version of *Amazing grace* have anything at all about ten thousand years?
12   Are the words and music clearly readable?
13   Does its version of *Thy/Your kingdom come, O God* include 'o'er heathen lands afar'?
14   Can the words be sung with integrity and conviction by your congregation?
15   Do more than 5% of first lines start with 'I'?
16   Is it a simple matter to find a hymn on the Transfiguration?
17   Do more than three tunes go above top E or below middle C?
18   Can you easily find a hymn by Anne Steele, Catherine Winkworth or Alan Gaunt?
19   Does the book include its own supplement bound in at the end?
20   Can you readily find a hymn connected with Psalm 98, Luke 13, or James 5?

Scoring

Even numbers: 10   Check again; there is no such book.
             7–9   This could be the one for you.
             <6   Hmm.

Odd numbers: 10   I hope there is no such book.
             6–9   Forget it.
             1–5   There may be something better.
             0   Ideal.

4

And Finally: News That Stays News!

Ezra Pound coined the phrase. As the centuries turn, we all seem less concerned with Ezra and more with the pound; but that poetically and politically ambiguous writer once described literature as 'news that stays news.' If that is a fair soundbite for classic prose and poetry, how much more is it true of the gospel of Christ! The task of hymns has always been to express, explore and respond to that good news, another deduction from our rare glimpse of the original hymn-singers in Colossians 3.16–17.

In the flood of backward looks and lists it was Simon Rae whose anthology of 'the 20th century in poems' (one per author, one per year) used Pound's phrase for his title and prompted my opening pages. His Introduction observes, 'Of course ability has not been spread evenly throughout the century'; the selection process 'has been fraught with invidious choices...even those who have ended up with a seat may cavil at the poem by which they are represented' (S Rae, ed, *News That Stays News*, London: Faber and Faber, 1999). So here. In our overlapping world of hymns we have no laureates, few heroes; Chesterton appears in both lists, but Norman Nicholson (who might have done) in neither. Simon Rae includes Auden and R S Thomas.

The AD2000 nostalgia industry seems rivalled only by that of forecasting. If our world lasts long enough to provide a similar booklet for the 21st century, its contrasts will be greater than anything within the 20th. Dare we predict that more people, not less, may be aware of hymns a hundred years on, though the way we select and display them may be unrecognizable?

As I struggled one afternoon through the concrete approaches of the University of Essex, I asked a stranger (who turned out to be a sociology lecturer) for directions. He was momentarily stunned to hear that I was searching for the Conference of the Hymn Society—even, in this day and age, that there was such a body. He mentally bracketed us with the Flat Earthers. What would he think if he read in the latest relevant American book (*A Survey of Christian Hymnody*, 4th edn, Carol Stream: Hope, 1999, p vii): 'Hymnology is a vast and rapidly growing field of study'?

And not merely study, since the researchers and courses cover not only history but contemporary Christianity—not what we *sang* but what we *sing*. Since becoming largely self-employed in 1995, I have attended nearly seventy Anglican and more than twenty-five Free churches, most in England, mostly not 'up front.' What we sing brings much delight, discovery, encouragement—and concern. But what *shall* we sing? Real hymns must fight the good fight!

David Wright is one of a growing group of Christians concerned for real hymns. 'Each generation needs to discover treasures from the past,' he says, 'as well as expressing concepts in contemporary language. But this will happen only if those who value good hymns promote their use effectively. Good real hymns can be a means of coming to faith, of building faith and of expressing faith; a means of prayer and of praise...Can we unite in finding and sharing ways to encourage the singing of good real hymns in the new Millennium?' (see also *News of Hymnody* No 73, Jan 2000).

My first 'Grove' title ended with a question-mark. This final page of my second deserves to end with a united exclamation: Amen! And for a coda, a text which fits PACHELBEL but which invites both a new tune and a renewed journey:

> We have not walked these paths before,
> nor viewed the scenes that meet our eyes;
> what fresh perspectives are in store,
> horizons hard to recognise
> that catch our breath with swift surprise.
>
> New sounds, new songs excite our ears,
> new needs are stretching heart and mind,
> unknown sensations, joys or fears;
> as passing fashions fall behind,
> what words, what wonders shall we find?
>
> And God who formed the ancient dust
> and wove the tapestry of space
> is far beyond, and wise and just,
> yet walks beside us at our pace;
> such is the mystery, such the grace.
>
> This much we know: here Jesus stood,
> and finished what he came to do,
> for all he did was wholly good
> and all he said was fully true,
> and what he makes is always new.
>
> For though our knowledge is but small,
> our faltering wisdom, feebler still,
> he lives, who made and knows us all,
> who met our evils, bore our ill,
> and beckons from the misty hill.

1st January 2000